About this Learning Guide

Shmoop Will Make You a Better Lover*
*of Literature, History, Poetry, Life...

Our lively learning guides are written by experts and educators who want to show your brain a good time. Shmoop writers come primarily from Ph.D. programs at top universities, including Stanford, Harvard, and UC Berkeley.

Want more Shmoop? We cover literature, poetry, bestsellers, music, US history, civics, biographies (and the list keeps growing). Drop by our website to see the latest.

www.shmoop.com

Table of Contents

Introduction

In a Nutshell

If you're not familiar with Wilfred Owen, don't worry, Shmoop is here to help. Though you may not have heard of Owen, he set the tone for an entire generation of men and women writing and thinking about the events that just rocked the world – World War I.

Between 1914 and 1918, over nine million people died. Entire cities were razed to the ground. Nations crumbled, only to be re-formed amidst political turmoil and enough bad blood to launch another war World War II, to be precise) a few short decades later. American troops joined the war in 1918, bringing with them the deadliest weapon yet: influenza. More people died of flu than war injuries.

Caught in a war that was waged primarily in trenches (big ditches that filled with mud, rats, and rainwater), Owen began to find it hard to justify all the suffering and death he witnessed. He was perfectly willing to sacrifice his life for king and country, but, like many other people, he'd like to make sure that his sacrifice was actually *needed*.

Increasingly convinced that the war seemed to be carrying on beyond the point of reason, Owen began to write poetry that emphasized the irony of his situation. He was in good company: as it turned out, *lots* of men (including Rupert Brooke, Siegfried Sassoon, John McCrae, and others) were feeling like their lives in the trenches were becoming farcical. Owen, however, managed to capture the division between the elevated language of nationalism and *his* reality, a world that suddenly seemed full of the blood of his nearest friends. Owen's experience rang true to a lot of the servicemen and women who contributed to the war efforts of the time.

Owen's gripping realism remains important today because, well, it's so *real*. When we read his poetry, we feel as though we're with him on the field, watching as men suffer in a frantic struggle to stay alive.

Why Should I Care?

Let's face it, there are many people out there who write about war. In addition to the news, there are blogs, journals, memoirs, radio shows, and video games that commemorate, re-live, or even celebrate the action of the war zone.

After the press is done talking and the bloggers stop blogging, however, do we really know what it's like out there on battlefields? Unless you've been in through it yourself, or have a friend or family member in the Armed Forces, chances are you don't.

Well, that's where Owen comes in. See, soldiers in World War I may not have had the technology of today's troops, but they probably share similar fears and even similar pain. At first glance, this poem may seem vehemently anti-war – but it actually directs most of its bitterness at the people who rally around the troops without ever understanding exactly *what* they're sending those troops off to do. Owen spent years on the battlefields. By most standards, he has earned the right to call it like he sees it.

Reading "Dulce et Decorum Est" may not be a walk in the park. But Owen's struggling with a difficult issue: he's trying to get a country to pay attention to the fact that people are dying. Whether or not you support of a particular war (or even war in general), it might be a good idea to listen to what he has to say.

The Poem

You can find "Dulce et Decorum Est" on Poets.org. (http://www.poets.org/viewmedia.php/prmMID/19389)

Overview and Line-by-Line Summary

Brief Summary

It's just another day on the battlefields of World War I . As our speaker lets us know right away, however, "normal" isn't a word that has any meaning for the soldiers anymore. They're all mentally and physically ravaged by the exertions of battle.

And then it gets worse. Just as the men are heading home for the night, gas shells drop beside them. The soldiers scramble for their gas masks in a frantic attempt to save their own lives. Unfortunately, they don't all get to their masks in time. Our speaker watches as a member of his crew chokes and staggers in the toxic fumes, unable to save him from an excruciating certain death.

Now fast-forward. It's some time after the battle, but our speaker just can't get the sight of his dying comrade out of his head. The soldier's image is everywhere: in the speaker's thoughts, in his dreams, in his poetry. Worst of all, our speaker can't do anything to help the dying soldier.

Bitterly, the speaker finally addresses the people at home who rally around the youth of England, and urge them to fight for personal glory and national honor. He wonders how they can continue to call for war. If they could only witness the physical agony war creates – or even experience the emotional trauma that the speaker's going through now – the speaker thinks they might change their views. In the speaker's mind, there's noting glorious or honorable about death. Or, for that matter, war itself.

Stanza I

Lines 1-2

Bent double, like old beggars under sacks,
Knock-kneed, coughing like hags, we cursed through sludge,

- The soldiers in this poem are crippled, mentally and physically overcome by the weight of their experiences in war.
- Did you notice how unwilling our speaker seems to introduce himself (and his fellow soldiers)? We're almost all the way through the second line before we (the readers) hear who "we" (the subjects of the poem) actually are.
- In fact, we get simile upon simile before we are acquainted with the subjects of this poem.
- We hear that they're "like old beggars" and "like hags."
- The speaker's searching for images that his reader can understand, as if he's convinced that none of his readers will be able to understand how horribly twisted and deformed the bodies of the soldiers have become.

Lines 3-4

Till on the haunting flares we turned our backs
And towards our distant rest began to trudge.

- The battle's about to end for the day.
- The soldiers turn away from the lights and noise of war and head back in the direction of their camp.
- There's an oh-so-subtle irony in the reference to the soldiers' "distant rest" (4).
- Sure, he *could* be talking about the barracks to which we guess that they're headed.
- Then again, they're soldiers in a war that wiped out over nine million men. Nine million.
- The "distant rest" to which our soldiers are heading may just be death.
- Trudging through the sludge is a pretty decent description of the trench warfare that became the battle plan for much of the First World War.
- Check out our "Best of the Web" links for detailed analyses of how disgusting and awful the trenches were.

Line 5

Men marched asleep.

- Zombies.
- Owen's opting for concise realism here: there's no need to fancy up the language of the poem.
- The horror of men walking as if they were dead (out of exhaustion, we're guessing) says it all.
- By ending a sentence in the middle of line five, Owen creates a caesura (a pause in the line), a formal effect that underscores the terseness of the poem's language at this point.

Lines 5-6

Many had lost their boots
But limped on, blood-shod.

- We mentioned that these guys seem a bit otherworldly before, but we'll say it again.
- Notice how lines 5-6 collect lots of "l" sounds? Words like "lost" and "limped" and "blood" all roll on our tongues, making the experience of reading the lines seem even lllonger.
- It's all part of Owen's technical dexterity: he's trying to get us to *feel* how interminable the soldiers' march seems right now.
- Also notice that the blood that has been shed seems to clothe them now, (or at least their feet). This creates a vivid image suggesting that the war – figuratively and literally – is enveloping their very beings.

Lines 6-8

All went lame; all blind;
Drunk with fatigue; deaf even to the hoots
Of tired, outstripped Five-Nines that dropped behind.

- Once again, the choppiness of lines 6-7 mimics the terseness of tired men.
- The rhythm of the lines even sounds a bit like the tramp of men marching in rhythm.
- Plus the repetition of "l"s continues.
- Notice how we've moved beyond the elaborate similes at the beginning of this stanza.
- Our speaker's not worried about comparing his comrades to things that the folks at home can understand.
- Worn out by the march, he's content to speak in sweeping observations.
- *All* the men are rendered disabled by the traumas that they've experienced.
- Maybe this isn't exactly an accurate historical account of a soldier's life in the war.
- After all, *all* of the men can't be lame and blind, can they? Or…can they?
- Perhaps the "drunk" and "deaf" soldiers might be temporarily overwhelmed by the never-ending strains of battle.
- Even the shells seem "tired" and "outstripped."
- (Five-Nines are gas shells. We'll hear lots more about them later.)
- The whole war, in other words, seems worn out.

Stanza II

Lines 9-10

Gas! Gas! Quick, boys! – An ecstasy of fumbling,
Fitting the clumsy helmets just in time;

- The repetition of a frantic cry, "Gas! Gas! Quick, boys!—" draws us straight into a frenzy of action.
- We're in the midst of an "ecstasy" of fumbling for helmets and gas masks.
- (If you're wondering just how nasty and terrifying gas attacks were, check out some of the historical links in our "Websites" section. Believe us, on a nastiness scale of 1 to 10, we put gas attacks at 10.5.)
- Does the word "ecstasy" seem strange here? It does to us.
- We're guessing that Owen's trying to draw upon an apocalyptic language: at the end of the world, just about anything that you're doing will probably seem ecstatic.
- The "ecstasy of fumbling" which goes on here, however, is anything but rapturous.
- We're back to the sort of ironic language that we've seen in the title – combining elevated language with absolute chaos makes the whole experience seem totally out of proportion.

Lines 11-12

But someone still was yelling out and stumbling
And flound'ring like a man in fire or lime...

- The eeriness of this line might have something to do with the fact that we don't know who the "someone" stumbling about in the night actually is.
- Notice how the verbs here have changed: our speaker's no longer describing universal conditions that could apply to anyone.
- He's in the moment, watching as a man is "stumbling" and "yelling" and "floundering."
- Those "–ing" conjugations of verbs create a sense of immediacy.
- The man's out there right now. His actions occur as we speak.
- As we say in our "Quotes" section, lime, or quicklime, is a chemical compound that can burn through the human body (sort of like fire).
- In other words, whatever the gas is doing to that man out there, it's awful.
- It's so awful that our speaker can't face it head-on: he has to describe it through similes, (like those similes we talked about in the first lines).

Lines 13-14

Dim, through the misty panes and thick green light,
As under a green sea, I saw him drowning.

- The repetition of the word "green" here allows our sense of the scene to fold in upon itself, almost as if the fog of green stuff is surrounding us as well.
- The long "ee"s of green lengthen the time it takes us to read the lines, slowing our tongues down slightly.
- It's like those scenes in horror movies that suddenly shift into slow motion: what's going on here is so awful that we have to pause in order to take it all in.

Stanza III

Lines 15-16
In all my dreams, before my helpless sight,
He plunges at me, guttering, choking, drowning.

- What's with the fact that these two lines form their own stanza? Shouldn't they be part of the second stanza?
- We don't have a solid lock on Owen's intentions here, of course, but here's what the poem itself tells us: this stanza fits into the rhyme scheme of stanza two.
- In fact, it's almost like Owen snapped it off of the second stanza and pushed it down the page a little ways.
- Why? Well, for one thing, these two lines bring us *out* of a past experience (the experience of the gas attack) and *into* a horrific present.
- In some ways, the present is a lot like the past – after all, all our speaker can think about is the gas attack.
- In others, however, it's a marked shift in the momentum of the poem.
- We can't think of the dying soldier as part of the past, if only because he plays such a huge role in our speaker's present.
- "All" his dreams have been taken over by a nightmarish memory of the gas attack.
- Notice now how the speaker seems to be directly involved in the man's suffering: in lines 14-15, watching through "dim" light as his comrade goes down.
- By the time we get to line 16, however, the other soldier "plunges" directly *at* our speaker. Moreover, the helplessness of our speaker takes center stage.
- He can't *do anything*. He can only replay the horrors of the scene, turning them over and over in his mind.
- It's almost as if using the word "drowning" at the end of line 15 triggered our speaker's memory, making him re-hash the horrors that he's witnessed.
- "Drowning" occurs again in line 17. In fact, it actually rhymes with itself.

Stanza IV

Lines 17-18
If in some smothering dreams you too could pace
Behind the wagon that we flung him in,

- Ah, now we get to the "you."
- Are we the audience to whom Owen addresses this poem?
- We're not quite sure.
- Several earlier versions of this poem were explicitly addressed to "Miss Pope," or Jessie Pope, a British propagandist who printed public letters urging men to take up arms in defense of their country's honor.

- Owen could be addressing the poem specifically to her.
- For the sake of argument, though, let's see what happens if our speaker's "you" is supposed to be us (the readers).
- If we accept that we're the people to whom our speaker addresses himself, something interesting happens: we're told that we *can't* understand what's going on in the poem…even as the speaker *tells* us what's going on.
- In fact, it's like a story that your friend might tell you. They might try to describe something that happened, but then end by saying, "you just had to be there."
- These lines actually take it a step further, though: our speaker doesn't even care whether we *could* actually experience the horrors of battle or not.
- He *knows* that we can't share those experiences with him.
- He's just wishing that we could share the *dreams* of the experiences of battle, but we can't do that.
- Such deliberate distancing of the speaker from the "you" of the poem creates a huge gap of isolation in which our speaker dwells.
- We just can't understand how horrible his life was…and is.

Lines 19-20

And watch the white eyes writhing in his face,
His hanging face, like a devil's sick of sin;

- We're still in the land of hypotheticals here.
- Our speaker's going into detail, forcing "you" (or, well, us) to imagine just how horrible his dreams can be.
- The body of the dream-soldier writhes in surreal agony.
- It's almost over-the-top, unless, of course, you've read descriptions of the pain and suffering of gas victims.
- Notice all the "s" sounds stacking up in the last line? (For starters, there's "fa**ce**" and "devil'**s**" and "**s**ick" and "**s**in.")
- When you read line 20 aloud, it's almost as if you're hissing your way through the line.
- The fancy technical term for repeating "s" sounds is sibilance…it's what snakes do.
- (And devils, if you take John Milton's word for it. Describing a devil by using an aural technique that forces the reader to hiss? That's pretty darn cool.)

Lines 21-24

If you could hear, at every jolt, the blood
Come gargling from the froth-corrupted lungs,
Obscene as cancer, bitter as the cud
Of vile, incurable sores on innocent tongues,–

- This is pretty disgusting.
- And that's our speaker's point.
- He wants to ram home just how absolutely degrading, humiliating, and surreal the

destruction of the human body can be.

- Within minutes, the body of a young man turns into a mass of aging sores – almost as a version of cancer moved through his body at warp speed.
- Owen takes on a bitter, ceaseless realism towards the end of this stanza.
- His speaker is deep in the memory of his own dream – and he's dragging us along for the ride.

Lines 25-27

My friend, you would not tell with such high zest
To children ardent for some desperate glory,
The old Lie:

- Now we get to the serious teeth of this poem: after drawing us deep into the hell of his personal experiences, our speaker lashes out at the those who helped get him into this mess.
- As he bitterly reflects, the war efforts begin at home.
- Lots of people are willing to convince young (and, he suggests, gullible) "children" that they can find glory on the battlefield.
- When you compare the heightened rhetoric or ("high zest") of these "patriots" to the stark realism of the lines preceding it, the difference between the two seems almost farcical.
- Owen sets up an implicit comparison between personal experience and national rhetoric.
- It's almost like we see two separate versions of war being fought: the one that's full of "glory" and "honor," and the other that breaks men in to "hags" and hallucinations.

Lines 27-28

Dulce et decorum est
Pro patria mori.

- If you haven't buffed up on Latin lately, don't worry. Your friendly Shmoop translation team is here to help.
- These Latin lines are quoted from Horace (a Roman philosopher and poet).
- Here's the lines in English: "It is sweet and proper to die for one's country."
- After reading all of the stuff that our speaker (and our speaker's comrade) have gone through, it's pretty hard to believe that Horace actually knows what he's talking about.
- We're guessing that that's Owen's point.
- Notice how the last line of the poem doesn't have anywhere close to ten syllables?
- For readers accustomed to seeing or hearing a line that's ten syllables long, this would sound like a huge, awkward silence.
- Maybe like the silence of death.

Technique

Symbols, Imagery, & Wordplay

Welcome to the land of symbols, imagery, and wordplay. Before you travel any further, please know that there may be some thorny academic terminology ahead. Never fear, Shmoop is here. Check out our "How to Read a Poem" section for a glossary of terms.

Disfiguration

Even before the shells drop and the world turns into a living nightmare, Owen concentrates on the ways that bodies get warped by the war. Emphasizing the ways in which men break under the stresses of war, our speaker creates a battle zone peopled by the walking dead.

- Line 1: "Bent double, like old beggars under sacks" is a simile, which compares the men marching to beggars. Starting the poem off with an image of men "doubled" creates the possibility that the soldiers really have become two people: the men they were before the war and the creatures that they are now.
- Line 2: More similes. This time the men are "Knock-kneed, coughing like hags." How do we know it's a simile? Well, it's a comparison that's created by using the word "like" to link the subject (the marching men) to another term (the hags).
- Line 5: "Men marched asleep." Line five starts out with a stark image. People don't usually walk in their sleep, unless something is seriously wrong. Making abnormality the norm seems to be one of the major functions of this war.
- Line 6: The parallel construction of the lines "All went lame; all blind;" emphasizes misery as a universal condition. No one escapes. No one.
- Line 15: The speaker's reference to his "helpless sight" creates an almost paradoxical image: his sight works well. After all, he *can* see the image of the man dying – in fact, it's our speaker's all-to-active sight, which becomes the problem. What Owen is actually describing, however, is the helplessness of the speaker himself. If that's the case, then "sight" functions as a synecdoche, standing in for the speaker as a whole.
- Line 18: The imagery created by describing "the white eyes writhing in [a soldier's] face" is horrendous. It's almost like the eyes have lives of their own: they've detached from the working of the body as a whole.
- Lines 21-24: Owen is racking up some serious imagery points here. From gargling blood to cancer-like sores, we've got it all. This poem is a true house of horrors. We get to witness as a soldier's body breaks down entirely.

Allusion

Although we don't get too many allusions, the ones we do get are central to the message of the poem. In fact, we begin and end with a shout-out to one of the founding fathers of Western literature, Horace. Why? Well, that's a good question….

- Line 2: The simile comparing soldiers to old hags has potential as an allusion as well. Think about it: literature is chock-full of nasty old hags. There's the witch in "Hansel and Gretel" and the witches of *Macbeth*. Even the old crone who helps the Sheriff of Nottingham in *Robin Hood: Prince of Thieves* could probably fall into the "hag" category.

Owen probably knew that his description would carry lots of cultural weight and used it to his advantage. Why compare soldiers to witches? Well, we'll leave that up to you.

- Line 20: The devil's always a popular allusion in poems about bad stuff. Frankly, he's about as bad as it gets.
- Lines 27-28: Ah, the biggie. This is the allusion to beat all allusions. It's one of the most-quoted lines of 20th century poetry…and Owen didn't even write it himself! Referring to a popular school text allows Owen to take a swing at all the popular rhetoric about the glories of war.

Nightmares

Just how "real" is this war scene that we're reading about? Well, that's a tricky question. For our speaker, it's too horrible to seem real at all. That's why we get so many descriptions of the battlefield as a bad dreamscape (you know, like one of those horrible night terrors that you had as a kid). The only difference is that you could wake up sweating and run to your parents. For this guy, the dream is the real deal.

- Line 2: See our analysis in "Allusion" of the simile comparing hags to soldiers here. If hags are witches, then they fit pretty well into the whole nightmare vibe that's being created.
- Line 2: Check out the alliteration in this line: the repeated "k" sounds begin to have an echoing quality, like the words that bounce around in a nightmarish fog.
- Lines 13-14: The imagery of these lines is pretty intense. Murky green lights and all-encompassing fog? Sounds scary to us.
- Lines 15-16: Here's where our speaker gets serious about his dreams. The image of the dying soldier becomes a literal nightmare, one which haunts the speaker for the rest of the poem.
- Line 19: This line is all alliteration all the time. The "w"s in this line just keep stacking up.
- Line 20: More sound play. Sibilance is the name of the game in this line: repeating "s" sounds create a sort of hissing on our tongues. Oh, and did we mention the allusion to the devil in this line? He's pretty nightmarish.

Form and Meter

Pentameter (most of the time)

We're pretty sure that you've heard of pentameter before. Remember Shakespeare? He set a pretty decent trend. Iambic pentameter became one of the most popular meters for poetry of all time. "Dulce et Decorum Est" follows in a long trend. Well, yes and no.

Don't worry – we'll explain.

The quick and dirty version of pentameter is this: there are ten beats or five "feet" (groupings of two syllables) in each line. Sound out the first line of this poem aloud – you'll see what we

mean.

Don't get too excited, though – "Dulce et Decorum Est" isn't your typical poem. In fact, it bucks the iambic pentameter trend. See, in iambic pentameter, every line should follow an unstressed/stressed syllable pattern. That's a complicated way of saying that when you speak the line, you're probably going to be emphasizing every other syllable. Here's an example from Shakespeare:

"When **for**/-ty **win**-/ters **shall**/ be-**siege**/ thy **brow**" (Sonnet 2.1)

Our poem, "Dulce et Decorum Est," doesn't follow this pattern. It's almost as if Owen is *pretending* to be conventional, only to explode all notions of conventional poetry from the inside. Sort of like the shells exploding over our speaker's head.

Likewise, the stanzas of "Dulce" disintegrate as the horrors of war start to mess with our speaker's mind. The first stanza falls into a pretty neat eight-line pattern: the ABABCDCD rhyme scheme divides the stanza neatly in two. When we get to the second (and third) stanzas, however, things begin to fall apart. Stanza two *seems* like it should follow the pattern laid out by the first stanza –after all, it has an ABABCD rhyme scheme, as well. The change in the rhyming pattern mirrors the increasing horrors of war.

Those of you who are good with numbers, though, will notice that stanza 2 only has six lines. In fact, its rhyme scheme breaks abruptly off, only to be continued in stanza 3. It's almost as if the stanza splits into two separate stanzas. Looking closely at the language of the poem, we can see why: the "drowning" that our speaker witnesses completely messes with his mind. He's so fixated on it, in fact, that he uses the same word, "drowning" to rhyme the end of stanza 2 with the end of stanza 3.

Once we get to the fourth (and final) stanza of this poem, all hell breaks loose. Sure, we're still in pentameter, but we've got twelve (count them: twelve) lines to deal with. And the last lines sure aren't in pentameter. It's almost as if the form mimics our speaker's inability to get the war out of his head. The poem just can't stop where it should…if only because our speaker can't seem to get himself out of the atrocities of the battleground.

Speaker

Remember Lieutenant Dan in *Forrest Gump*? He's from a later war, but we're betting that his tone is pretty much the voice in your head when you read "Dulce et Decorum Est." Before he gets on the shrimp boat with Forrest, he's a bitter and broken man. He just can't figure out how the world could deal him this hand of cards, or why no one, not even his best friends, can seem to understand the horror that he's experienced.

That bitterness tracks well into this poem, which savagely attacks those back home who incite innocent young boys to fight impossible and unending battles. As far as our speaker is concerned, a few lines of poetry aren't going to compensate for the fact that your friend has been killed, or that he continues to haunt your nightmares.

Like Wilfred Owen, our speaker is up on his Latin poetry. Strangely enough, reciting sections of Horace's *Odes* wasn't all *that* uncommon for the people during the war. Many people went to public school. (For folks in England, "public" school actually means private school. We're not really sure why.) Everyone who went to public school learned the same Latin poems and heard the same speeches about glory and honor. Because our speaker knows that his readers are the educated elite, he's got no problem tossing off quotes from Horace.

The speaker of this poem is also a soldier through and through. He's trudging with the sleeping men at the beginning of the poem and he's dreaming about the same men at the poem's end. The center of the poem hinges on our speaker as a witness. As he says, "I saw him drowning" (14). Line 14 is the literal center of the poem. More importantly, it's the thematic heart of the poem, as well. The "drowning" of a man in gas fumes becomes the image that occupies our speaker for the rest of the poem.

In some ways, this scene of the poem is literally the *only* scene that matters to our speaker now. There's no way for him to move forward. He plays and re-plays the "smothering dreams" of battle in his head (17). Ironically, our speaker lets us see that the "men [who] marched asleep" had things pretty good: sure, their feet were bloody and their bodies torn up, but at least they could sleep in relative peace (5). Our fellow, on the other hand, can't sleep at all. His dreams might even be worse than the battle itself. Death is his constant companion. All that trauma would be enough to make anyone hate the warmongers at home.

Sound Check

This poem's not playing too many games with us. It's so deeply entrenched in the world of war that its language can't help but re-create the language and the pace of the battlefield. Starting the second stanza with a sharp cry, "Gas! Gas!" draws us smack-dab into the middle of the action (9). We're not worried about what the soldiers look like or sound like now. Thrown into a murky, misty green world of toxic fumes, we try as hard as our speaker does to make sense of language that seems to create a haze of frantic action.

Then again, there are some pretty masterful sleights-of-hand to pull straight into this world of war. Check out the first few lines of the poem: the repetition of hard consonant sounds like the hard "k" in "sacks," "knock," "coughed" and "cursed" makes our tongues perform some sharp attacks on the air in our mouths. If you listen closely, it might even sound vaguely like the machine-gun fire which was the sonic backdrop of the battlefield in World War I. Technically, that's alliteration. (Check out our "Symbols, Imagery, Wordplay" for a more detailed analysis of all the alliterative work that's going on in this poem.) For now, though, we'll say that the true-to-the-moment sound of this poem masks a technically adept poet at work.

Oh, and did we talk about the Latin? In case we didn't mention it, Latin's a dead language. It's not spoken. And it's a bit creepy to end with a language that is itself dead. So what do we make of the fact that you just can't *speak* the last lines of this poem? We'll analyze that in "Symbols, Imagery, Wordplay," as well – but it poses a problem to anyone who's "sounding" out this poem. How does one "speak" a language that's not spoken?

What's Up With the Title?

Owen starts out with some serious irony here. The title of his poem, "Dulce et Decorum Est," is actually a reference to one of Horace's *Odes*. (By the way, Horace was a Roman philosopher and poet.) The translated version might look something like this: "It is sweet and proper." We get a fuller version of the title in the last stanza of the poem. (Check out our "Detailed Summary" for a reading of this longer version.)

Hmm…something's not right here. Can it really be "sweet and proper" for men to "march asleep?" Or for soldiers to march so long and fight so hard that they no longer resemble men at all? The "beggars" and "hags" of the first stanza sure don't seem like prime candidates for people that you'd want up on a national platform on Memorial Day.

Maybe that's Owen's point. Irony is a major mode for this poem. It's *not* proper and it's sure not sweet to become "bent double" and "knock-kneed" (1,2). And we haven't even begun to talk about what happens when gas shells begin to drop.

Owen grew up in Britain in the early twentieth century, when most schoolchildren got a good smattering of Latin in their education, especially if they went to parochial schools. Horace's *Odes* were frequently read by schoolchildren – a point that certainly doesn't escape our author's attention. Kids are taught that dying in battle is a brave and honorable thing to do. After all, that's how heroes are made, right?

In Owen's opinion, this couldn't be further from the truth. Emphasizing the gruesome details of his real experiences during the war allows him to demonstrate the emptiness of war. If schoolbooks teach us what heroes ought to do, his poem seeks to show us just how un-heroic wartime action can be.

Calling Card

Death. Lots and Lots of Death.

OK, so Wilfred Owen doesn't have a lock on death. After all, pretty much every major novelist and/or poet who's ever written anything has something to say on the subject. For Owen, however, death is *the* subject. In the tumult of battle, only one thing is certain: somebody will die. During the war, even the men who are alive act like zombies. If you've watched *Sean of the Dead*, you know that "zombie" is a another word for the walking dead. Given that Owen's poetry is all written during World War I, we're betting that he didn't have much opportunity to write about other material. Death may not be easy to face – but that, friends, is Owen's point.

Tough-O-Meter

(3) Base Camp

Owen's trying to make us feel like we're actually with him on the battlefield as the gas shells are dropping. There's a bit of confusion in all the smoke and haze and chaos and destruction, but the poem itself remains remarkably clear. We're with him as his friend's face melts in front of him. We're even with him when that face dances beside his bedside at night. It might not be a pretty picture, but it's a pretty easy one to get. We're guessing that's because he doesn't want anyone to miss his point: war is hell.

Setting

The Battlefields of World War I

Seeing through the "misty panes and thick green light" of a world suddenly turned upside-down by the dropping of gas shells, we're dragged through horrors that seem too terrible to be real, and too real to be anything but first-hand experience (13). It's a world peopled by the walking dead. Soldiers tramp through mud and gore, their own bodies falling apart as they move slowly towards their tents. Even the flares overhead (thrown to alert bombers about potential targets) are "haunting," suggesting that the battlefield itself may be one step closer to the afterlife than even the soldiers would like to think. Owen describes the scene as incredibly gruesome, and he's more than willing to walk us through it in excruciating detail.

By the end of the poem, we seem to have moved off the actual battlefield, or have we? The poem turns inward, becoming a mindscape of the speaker's nightmares. Because we've already gotten a good sense of just how nightmarish actual battle scenes are, however, the difference between the speaker's mind and a minefield doesn't seem to be that great.

It's a clever move on Owen's part: there's no difference between the awful scenes of wartime and the traumatized mind of a soldier *after* battle because the soldier's mind never leaves the battlefield. See how crafty that is? When our speaker cries out, "In all my dreams, before my helpless sight, He plunges at me, guttering, choking, drowning," we can't tell whether he's still in the war or looking back on his experiences months (or years) afterwards. There are some settings that you just can't get out of your system.

Themes

Theme of Warfare

As Owen describes it, war becomes a never-ending nightmare of muddy trenches and unexpected gas attacks. Interestingly, with the new-fangled technology of WWI, there doesn't even need to be a real enemy present to create the devastation and destruction. Set in the

middle of a gas attack, this poem explores the intense agony of a world gone suddenly insane – and the unfortunate men who have to struggle through it. As the poem itself asks, how can anyone condone so much suffering?

Questions About Warfare

1. Does the description of battle in this poem seem realistic? Can you easily imagine it? Why or why not?
2. Do you have any sense of why the soldiers in this poem are fighting?
3. Describe the most vivid images in this poem. Are they actually battle-images?
4. Whom does the speaker blame for the continuance of the war?

Chew on this: Warfare

"Dulce et Decorum Est" becomes a chronicle of the living dead: the soldiers whose minds remain trapped in the horrors of battle.

Theme of Suffering

Physical pain and psychological trauma blur in this searing description of a World War I battleground. Caught in the memory of a gas-attack, the poem's speaker oscillates between the pain of the past (the actual experience of battle) and the pain of the present (he can't get the image of his dying comrade out of his head). As Owen argues, war is so painful that it becomes surreal.

Questions About Suffering

1. Does the gassed soldier ever seem like a real character in this poem? Why or why not?
2. What formal devices does Owen use to make the suffering of soldiers seem realistic? (See our "Symbols, Imagery, Wordplay" section for some starting points.)
3. Who suffers more in this poem: the gassed soldier or the speaker?
4. Which is more important: the loss of innocence or the loss of bodily integrity? What in the text allows you to draw your conclusion?

Chew on this: Suffering

By drawing readers directly into the action of battle, Owen's speaker manipulates us into assuming the anti-war stance that results from his own experiences of the war.

Theme of Patriotism

In this poem, dying for your country (or even fighting for your country) seems a lot less worthwhile than the trumped-up truisms of old patriotic battle cries imply. Strategically drawing his readers through the ghastly reality of life in a battle zone, Owen turns patriotic fervor into a kind of deadly life force. The people at home just can't understand how horrible life on the front actually is. The soldiers in war can't remember why they are fighting. Everyone, it seems, is lost: lost in a fog of war or in the useless ideals that sacrifice youth at the altar of national glory.

Questions About Patriotism

1. Why doesn't Owen insert a wartime slogan in English? What does the Latin quote in the poem's last lines add to the overall effect of poem?
2. Is there a difference between the "boys" in battle and the "children" in the last stanza?
3. Is Owen's poem unpatriotic? Why or why not?
4. What is the poem's attitude towards civilian opinions of the war? How can you tell?

Chew on this: Patriotism

"Dulce et Decorum Est" privileges individual well-being (or ending individual suffering) over the collective good.

Theme of Versions of Reality

"Dulce et Decorum Est" creates a sharp and deeply ironic line between the civilians who prop up war efforts and the men who fight their battles. As Owen suggests, there's almost no way for either group to understand the other. Only those who have experienced the horror of battle can understand the trauma of losing a fellow soldier. Ironically, however, these soldiers don't have the ability to communicate fully with those at home who *could* bring the war to an end – the people who reiterate old slogans about honor, duty, and patriotism without ever having to experience the terror of battle themselves. The very word "war" begins to mean two very different things for the two populations in this poem. Tragically, these views seem increasingly irreconcilable.

Questions About Versions of Reality

1. Who is the "you" to whom the speaker addresses the poem?
2. Which is scarier: the battle itself or the dreams of battle the speaker later experiences? How does the language of the poem help you reach this conclusion?
3. What sort of picture of war do the last lines of the poem create? How does the rest of the poem undercut this viewpoint?

Chew on this: Versions of Reality

Through emphasis on the hellish, nightmarish quality of gas-attacks, Owen suggests that war itself is a vain dream.

Quotes

Warfare Quotes

"...deaf even to the hoots
Of tired, outstripped Five-Nines that dropped behind" (7-8).

Thought: "Five-Nines" are gas shells, the dropping of which starts off the action of the rest of the poem. The fact that even the shells seem "tired" and "outstripped" suggests that the war might be dragging on too long.

"Gas! Gas! Quick, boys! – An ecstasy of fumbling,
Fitting the clumsy helmets just in time;" (9-10)

Thought: The exclamations at the beginning of line 9 speed up the pace of the poem, bringing us into the action with all the drama that the soldiers themselves experience. The hyphen in the middle of the line reinforces this urgency, moving through the pause in the middle of the line as if it, too, is suddenly sped up.

Men marched asleep. (5)

Thought: War seems like a continual process in this line: even when the men are "sleeping," they're advancing or retreating from the field of battle. The image as a whole contributes to the ghost-like quality of the soldiers in this poem.

"Many had lost their boots
But limped on, blood-shod. All went lame; all blind;" (5-6)

Thought: The trench warfare of WWI caused lots of soldiers' legs to rot. Literally. Mired in mud and gore, the soldiers often had to spend hours (if not days) standing in trenches. The detailed description of *how* men come to be wounded is followed by sweeping statements about the condition of all soldiers.

"If in some smothering dreams you too could pace
Behind the wagon that we flung him in," (17-18)

Thought: Owen's phrasing here is intentionally vague: does the experience seem like a "smothering dream" to those who are living it, or would the reader have to enter into a dream-state in order to understand it?

Suffering Quotes

"Bent double, like old beggars under sacks,
Knock-kneed, coughing like hags, we cursed through sludge," (1-2)

Thought: The bodies of the soldier are twisted and contorted, making their experience seem completely different from the sorts of marching that we usually see in military parades. Here they're like "beggars" and "hags" – cast-off elements of society.

Men marched asleep. (5)

Thought: Ok, maybe sleeping is the best thing that people can do in the midst of all this trudging through mud and bullets - but sleep deprivation can't be all that pleasant. Unfortunately, in this poem, it's the least of the speaker's worries.

"Many had lost their boots
But limped on, blood-shod. All went lame; all blind;
Drunk with fatigue; deaf even to the hoots
Of tired, outstripped Five-Nines that dropped behind." (5-8)

Thought: Words like "lame," "blind," "drunk" and "deaf" suggest that the soldiers have been stripped of their bodily integrity before they even enter into battle. They're almost zombie-men, stumbling through the dark with bodies that don't work anymore. And that's before the gas attack.

"But someone still was yelling out and stumbling
And flound'ring like a man in fire or lime..." (11-12)

Thought: Lime, or quicklime, is a chemical compound that can burn through the human body (sort of like fire). Referring to death by fire or lime allows Owen to describe the horrors of gassing as both natural and unnatural suffering…it's like fire and lime-burns combined.

"In all my dreams, before my helpless sight,
He plunges at me, guttering, choking, drowning." (15-16)

Thought: Because the trio of verbs in line 17 are gerunds (verb forms that end in –ing), we get the sense that the action is in the present tense. The speaker's comrade dies over and over in his dream, making the suffering of wartime casualties never-ending.

"…the white eyes writhing in his face,
His hanging face, like a devil's sick of sin;" (17-18)

Thought: The man described here seems almost inhuman…as if the physical effects of gassing can transform his body into a version of hell on earth. His very face begins to melt off of him.

"If you could hear, at every jolt, the blood
Come gargling from the froth-corrupted lungs,
Obscene as cancer, bitter as the cud
Of vile, incurable sores on innocent tongues,—" (21-24)

Thought: The intense imagery of these lines emphasizes how *un*imaginable such horrors are for the civilian population. No one can understand how excruciating it is to die of gas poisoning, unless, of course, you're watching your comrades choke on their own blood.

Patriotism Quotes

"My friend, you would not tell with such high zest
To children ardent for some desperate glory,
The old Lie: Dulce et decorum est
Pro patria mori." (25-28)

Thought: In this deeply ironic account of the efforts to get young men to enroll in the armed forces, the "zest" for patriotism and glory is undercut by all of the horrors that occur earlier in the poem. Owen's choice of the word "children" is an interesting one: it points to an innocence that will be lost forever once the "boys" step onto the battlefield.

"Dulce et decorum est
Pro patria mori." (27-28)

Thought: Read by schoolchildren throughout Britain, this excerpt from Horace's works can be translated as "It is sweet and proper to die for one's country."

Versions of Reality Quotes

"Bent double, like old beggars under sacks,
Knock-kneed, coughing like hags, we cursed through sludge," (1-2)

Thought: Using the word "like" to create two similes (the soldiers are "like" "old beggars" and "hags"), Owen suggests that their reality is so surreal that he needs to find comparative ways to describe it so that his readers can understand how gruesome his experience has been.

"Dim, through the misty panes and thick green light,
As under a green sea, I saw him drowning." (13-14)

Thought: The many veils between the speaker and the dying man create an otherworldly sense in these lines, almost as if the man is already in the underworld (or hell).

"In all my dreams, before my helpless sight,
He plunges at me, guttering, choking, drowning." (15-16)

Thought: After the events narrated in the poem, the speaker's dreams are as real (if not more real) than his waking experiences. The war becomes a mental battle, one which doesn't stop wrecking his mind even after the official fighting has ceased.

"If in some smothering dreams you too could pace
Behind the wagon that we flung him in,
And watch the white eyes writhing in his face,
His hanging face, like a devil's sick of sin;
If you could hear, at every jolt, the blood
Come gargling from the froth-corrupted lungs,
Obscene as cancer, bitter as the cud
Of vile, incurable sores on innocent tongues,—" (17-24)

Thought: Starting this stanza with "if" allows the speaker to subtly point out the distance between himself and his readers. We don't have smothering dreams. We can't hear the dying soldier's gasping breath. When we read the poem, we only experience these scenes as *conditional* descriptions. "If" we could see them, we might understand – but for the speaker, that seems to be a pretty big "if."

"My friend, you would not tell with such high zest
To children ardent for some desperate glory,
The old Lie:" (25-27)

Thought: Referring to the reader (or his intended audience) as a "friend" seems like an ironic move on the speaker's part. After all, it's the enthusiastic ignorance of the "friends" participating in war efforts at home which got the speaker into this horrible mess in the first place.

"…Dulce et decorum est
Pro patria mori." (27-28)

Thought: Why end with a quote in Latin? Well, for one thing, it's a direct quote from Horace. For another, it emphasizes the foreignness of such concepts as "patriotism" and "glory for one's country" on the battlefield. Once you get into the war, the speaker suggests, such words are nothing more than a dead language.

Study Questions

1. Why end the poem with a Latin quote? Why not an English slogan?
2. How would the poem be different if the last stanza weren't addressed to people at home? How does this stanza change the meaning of the poem?
3. Do you think that the speaker creates a realistic picture of his own experiences? Why or why not?
4. How would you characterize the speaker's attitude towards war?

Did You Know?

Trivia

- Believe it or not, poems don't spring fully formed from an author's brain. Check out the writing and revision process that Owen went through with "Dulce et Decorum Est" here: you can scroll through four different versions of the poem (in manuscript form) and see just how the masterpiece we read today was created.
- Apparently, 19th century university students changed Horace's quote into a drinking chant:

  "Dulce et decorum est pro patria mori,
  sed dulcius pro patria vivere,
  et dulcissimum pro patria bibere.
  Ergo, bibamus pro salute patriae"

  Roughly translated, that's: "It is sweet and proper to die for one's country, but it is sweeter to live for one's country, and it is the sweetest to drink for one's country. Therefore, let us drink to the health of our country." We can't verify this, but you can follow up on it here.

Steaminess Rating

G

When death and misery are all around, sex might just be the last thing on your mind. Or maybe the first. Who are we to judge? In this poem, however, the immediacy of battle drowns out all other thoughts.

Allusions and Cultural References

Literary and Philosophical References

- Horace, *Odes* (title, 27-28)

Historical References

- World War I (8,9) (title, 27-28)

Best of the Web

Videos

Life During a Gas Attack
http://www.bbc.co.uk/history/worldwars/wwone/launch_ani_wwone_movies.shtml
An animated account of experiencing a gas attack, complete with photos and first-hand testimony.

The Great War
http://www.pbs.org/greatwar/
This website builds upon the massive (and actually pretty interesting) documentary on WWI, *The Great War*. It's got lots of cool interactive tools, as well

Audio

The BBC reads Owen's "The Sentry"
http://www.bbc.co.uk/history/worldwars/wwone/wilfred_owen_gallery_01.shtml

We know this isn't the poem we're discussing – but everybody loves a good British accent, right?

Poems Aloud
http://www.eaglesweb.com/Sub_Pages/owen_poems.htm
Hey, why read aloud yourself when you can get someone else to do it for you?

Images
Gas Attack
http://www.firstworldwar.com/photos/graphics/cpe_liquid_fire_01.jpg
A photo of a gas attack.

Gas Masks
http://www.firstworldwar.com/photos/graphics/cnp_soldier_gasmask_01.jpg
Check out the WWI gas masks on these men.

Wilfred Owen
http://bluehydrangeas.files.wordpress.com/2006/09/wilfred-owen.jpg
A photo of the poet.

Historical Documents
For all you Latin junkies...
http://www.thelatinlibrary.com/hor.html
Check out Horace's original ode here.

All about World War I
http://www.bbc.co.uk/history/worldwars/wwone/
On the BBC's extensive website, you can find a ton of information about World War I – or any other war, for that matter.

All about Wilfred Own
http://www.bbc.co.uk/history/worldwars/wwone/wilfred_owen_gallery_01.shtml
As far as war celebrities go, Wilfred Owen's rather high on the list. Check out his info on the BBC's history site.

Books
The Regeneration Trilogy
http://www.amazon.com/Regeneration-Pat-Barker/dp/0452270073
Pat Barker's multiple Booker Award-winning novels are collected in this three-volume set. They're fictional accounts of Craiglockhart War Hospital, where Wilfred Owen spent a good deal of time. They're also darn good books.

The Collected Poems of Wilfred Owen
http://www.amazon.com/Collected-Poems-Wilfred-Owen-Directions/dp/0811201325/ref=sr_1_1
?ie=UTF8&s=books&qid=1225915734&sr=1-1
If "Dulce et Decorum Est" wasn't enough for you, check out one of these collections of Owen's

poetry.

Movies & TV
Wilfred Owen: a Remembrance Tale
http://www.imdb.com/title/tt1155600/
Part documentary, part re-enactment, this T.V. show does just what its title promises – it remembers Wilfred.

The Great War and the Shaping of the Twentieth Century
http://www.imdb.com/title/tt0115193/
An amazing PBS documentary about fighting wars.

Websites
All Wilfred, All the Time
http://www.hcu.ox.ac.uk/jtap/
The Wilfred Owen Multimedia Digital Archive includes links to just about everything that could ever have had anything to do with Wilfred Owen. We're not even kidding.

The Wilfred Owen Association
http://www.1914-18.co.uk/owen/
OK, so the layout's not so pretty – but this site does have some cool information. And lots of pictures of Owen's grave.

Shmoop's Poetry Primer

How to Read Poem

There's really only one reason that poetry has gotten a reputation for being so darned "difficult": it demands your full attention and won't settle for less. Unlike a novel, where you can drift in and out and still follow the plot, poems are generally shorter and more intense, with less of a conventional story to follow. If you don't make room for the *experience*, you probably won't have one.

But the rewards can be high. To make an analogy with rock and roll, it's the difference between a two and a half minute pop song with a hook that you get sick of after the third listen, and a slow-building tour de force that sounds fresh and different every time you hear it. Once you've gotten a taste of the really rich stuff, you just want to listen to it over and over again and figure out: how'd they do that?

Aside from its demands on your attention, there's nothing too tricky about reading a poem. Like anything, it's a matter of practice. But in case you haven't read much (or any) poetry before, we've put together a short list of tips that will make it a whole lot more enjoyable.

- **Follow Your Ears.** It's okay to ask, "What does it mean?" when reading a poem. But it's

even better to ask, "How does it sound?" If all else fails, treat it like a song. Even if you can't understand a single thing about a poem's "subject" or "theme," you can always say something – anything – about the sound of the words. Does the poem move fast or slow? Does it sound awkward in sections or does it have an even flow? Do certain words stick out more than others? Trust your inner ear: if the poem sounds strange, it doesn't mean you're reading it wrong. In fact, you probably just discovered one of the poem's secret tricks! If you get stuck at any point, just look for Shmoop's "Sound Check" section. We'll help you listen!

- **Read It Aloud.** OK, we're not saying you have to shout it from the rooftops. If you're embarrassed and want to lock yourself in the attic and read the poem in the faintest whisper possible, go ahead. Do whatever it takes, because reading even part of poem aloud can totally change your perspective on how it works.

- **Become an Archaeologist.** When you've drunk in the poem enough times, experiencing the sound and images found there, it is sometimes fun to switch gears and to become an archaeologist (you know -- someone who digs up the past and uncovers layers of history). Treat the poem like a room you have just entered. Perhaps it's a strange room that you've never seen before, filled with objects or people that you don't really recognize. Maybe you feel a bit like Alice in Wonderland. Assume your role as an archaeologist and take some measurements. What's the weather like? Are there people there? What kind of objects do you find? Are there more verbs than adjectives? Do you detect a rhythm? Can you hear music? Is there furniture? Are there portraits of past poets on the walls? Are there traces of other poems or historical references to be found? Check out Shmoop's "Setting," "Symbols, Imagery, Wordplay," and "Speaker" sections to help you get started.

- **Don't Skim.** Unlike the newspaper or a textbook, the point of poetry isn't to cram information into your brain. We can't repeat it enough: poetry is an experience. If you don't have the patience to get through a long poem, no worries, just start with a really short poem. Understanding poetry is like getting a suntan: you have to let it sink in. When you glance at Shmoop's "Detailed Summary," you'll see just how loaded each line of poetry can be.

- **Memorize!** "Memorize" is such a scary word, isn't it? It reminds us of multiplication tables. Maybe we should have said: "Tuck the poem into your snuggly memory-space." Or maybe not. At any rate, don't tax yourself: if you memorize one or two lines of a poem, or even just a single cool-sounding phrase, it will start to work on you in ways you didn't know possible. You'll be walking through the mall one day, and all of a sudden, you'll shout, "I get it!" Just not too loud, or you'll get mall security on your case.

- **Be Patient.** You can't really understand a poem that you've only read once. You just can't. So if you don't get it, set the poem aside and come back to it later. And by "later" we mean days, months, or even years. Don't rush it. It's a much bigger accomplishment to actually *enjoy* a poem than it is to be able to explain every line of it. Treat the first reading as an investment – your effort might not pay off until well into the future, but when it does, it will totally be worth it. Trust us.

- **Read in Crazy Places.** Just like music, the experience of poetry changes depending on your mood and the environment. Read in as many different places as possible: at the beach, on a mountain, in the subway. Sometimes all it takes is a change of scenery for a poem to really come alive.

- **Think Like a Poet.** Here's a fun exercise. Go through the poem one line at a time,

covering up the next line with your hand so you can't see it. Put yourself in the poet's shoes: If I had to write a line to come after this line, what would I put? If you start to think like this, you'll be able to appreciate all the different choices that go into making a poem. It can also be pretty humbling – at least we think so. Shmoop's "Calling Card" section will help you become acquainted with a poet's particular, unique style. Soon, you'll be able to decipher a T.S. Elliot poem from a Wallace Stevens poem, sight unseen. Everyone will be so jealous.

- **"Look Who's Talking."** Ask the most basic questions possible of the poem. Two of the most important are: "Who's talking?" and "Who are they talking to?" If it's a Shakespeare sonnet, don't just assume that the speaker is Shakespeare. The speaker of every poem is kind of fictional creation, and so is the audience. Ask yourself: what would it be like to meet this person? What would they look like? What's their "deal," anyway? Shmoop will help you get to know a poem's speaker through the "Speaker" section found in each study guide.

- And, most importantly, **Never Be Intimidated.** Regardless of what your experience with poetry in the classroom has been, no poet wants to make his or her audience feel stupid. It's just not good business, if you know what we mean. Sure, there might be tricky parts, but it's not like you're trying to unlock the secrets of the universe. Heck, if you want to ignore the "meaning" entirely, then go ahead. Why not?   If you're still feeling a little timid, let Shmoop's "Why Should I Care" section help you realize just how much you have to bring to the poetry table.

Poetry is about freedom and exposing yourself to new things. In fact, if you find yourself stuck in a poem, just remember that the poet, 9 times out of 10, was a bit of a rebel and was trying to make his friends look at life in a completely different way. Find your inner rebel too. There isn't a single poem out there that's "too difficult" to try out – right now, today. So hop to it. As you'll discover here at Shmoop, there's plenty to choose from.

Sources:

http://allpoetry.com/column/2339540
http://academic.reed.edu/writing/paper_help/figurative_language.html
http://web.uvic.ca/wguide/Pages/LiteraryTermsTOC.html#RhetLang
http://www.tnellen.com/cybereng/lit_terms/allegory.html

What is Poetry?

What is poetry? At the most basic level, poetry is an *experience* produced by two elements of language: "sense" and "sound." The "sense" of a word is its meaning. The word "cat" refers to a small, furry animal with whiskers, a long tail, and, if you're unlucky, a knack for scratching up all your new furniture. We can all agree that's what "cat" means. But "cat" also has a particular sound when you say it, and this sound is different from similar words for "cat" in other languages.

Most of the things that you hear, say, or read in your daily life (including the words you are reading right now) put more emphasis on meaning than on sound. Not so with poetry. Have you ever repeated a word so many times that it started to sound strange and foreign? No? Try saying that word "cat" twenty times in a row. "Cat, cat, cat, cat, cat, cat . . ." Kind of weird, right? Well, guess what: you just made poetry out of a single word – that is, you turned the word into an experience that is as much about sound as it is about sense. Congratulations, poet!

Or let's imagine that you type the words "blue" and "ocean" on a page all by their lonesome selves. These two little words are quite ordinary and pop up in conversations all the time. However, when we see them isolated, all alone on a page, they might just take on a whole new meaning. Maybe "blue ocean" looks like a little strand of islands in a big sea of white space, and maybe we start to think about just how big the ocean is. Or you could reverse the order and type the words as "ocean blue," which would bring up a slightly different set of connotations, such as everyone's favorite grade-school rhyme: "In 1492 Columbus sailed the ocean blue."

Poetry is also visual, and so it's a good idea to pay attention to how the words are assembled on the page. Our imaginations are often stirred by a poem's visual presentation. Just like a person, poems can send all kinds of signals with their physical appearance. Some are like a slick businessman in a suit or a woman in an evening gown. Their lines are all regularized and divided neatly into even stanzas. Others are like a person at a rock concert who is dressed in tattered jeans, a ragged t-shirt, and a Mohawk, and who has tattoos and piercings all over their body! And some poems, well, some poems look like a baked potato that exploded in your microwave. It's always a good idea to ask yourself how the appearance of words on the page interacts with the meaning of those words. If the poem is about war, maybe it looks like a battle is going on, and the words are fighting for space. If the poem is about love, maybe the lines are spaced to appear as though they are dancing with one another. Often the appearance and meaning will be in total contrast, which is just as interesting.

OK, that's a very broad idea of what poetry is. Let's narrow it down a bit. When most people talk about poetry, they are talking about a particular kind of literature that is broken up into lines, or *verses*. In fact, for most of history, works divided into verse were considered more "literary" than works in prose. Even those long stories called "epics," like Homer's *The Odyssey* and Virgil's *Aeneid*, are actually poems.

Now, you're thinking: "Wait a minute, I thought verses belong to songs and music." Exactly. The very first poets – from Biblical times and even before – set their poems to music, and it's still acceptable to refer to a poem as a "song." For example, the most famous work by the American poet Walt Whitman is titled, "Song of Myself." Because of their shared emphasis on sound, poetry and music have always been like blood brothers.

The last thing to say about poetry is that it doesn't like to be pinned down. That's why there's no single definition that fits all of the things that we would call "poems." Just when you think you have poetry cornered, and you're ready to define it as literature broken into lines, it breaks free and shouts, "Aha! You forgot about the *prose poem*, which doesn't have any verses!" Drats! Fortunately, we get the last laugh, because we can enjoy and recognize poems even without a perfect definition of what poetry is.

Sources:

http://allpoetry.com/column/2339540
http://academic.reed.edu/writing/paper_help/figurative_language.html
http://web.uvic.ca/wguide/Pages/LiteraryTermsTOC.html#RhetLang
http://www.tnellen.com/cybereng/lit_terms/allegory.html

Poetry Glossary

Allegory: An allegory is a kind of extended metaphor (a metaphor that weaves throughout the poem) in which objects, persons, and actions stand for another meaning.

Alliteration: Alliteration happens when words that begin with the same sound are placed close to one another. For example, "the **s**illy **s**nake **s**ilently **s**linked by" is a form of alliteration. Try saying that ten times fast.

Allusion: An allusion happens when a speaker or character makes a brief and casual reference to a famous historical or literary figure or event.

Anaphora: Anaphora involves the repetition of the same word or group of words at the beginning of successive clauses or sections. Think of an annoying kid on a road trip: "Are we there yet? / Are we going to stop soon? / Are we having lunch soon?". Not a poem we'd like to read in its entirety, but the repetition of the word "are" is anaphora.

Anthologize: To put in a poetry anthology, usually for teaching purposes, so that students have a broad selection of works to choose from. Usually, the word will come up in a context like this: "That's one of her most famous poems. I've seen it anthologized a lot." An anthology is a book that has samples of the work of a lot of different writers. It's like a plate of appetizers so you can try out a bunch of stuff. You can also find anthologies for different periods, like Romantic, Modern, and Postmodern. The Norton, Columbia, and Best American anthologies are three of the most famous.

Apostrophe: Apostrophe is when an idea, person, object, or absent being is addressed as if it or they were present, alive, and kicking. John Donne uses apostrophe when he writes this: "Death be not proud, though some have called thee / Mighty and dreadful."

Avant Garde: You'll hear this word used to describe some of the craziest, most far-out, experimental poets. It was originally a French expression that refers to the soldiers who go explore a territory before the main army comes in. Avant garde artists are often people who break through boundaries and do what's never been done before. Then again, sometimes there's a good reason why something has been done before…

Ballad: A ballad is a song: think boy bands and chest-thumping emotion. But in poetry, a ballad is ancient form of storytelling. In the (very) old days, common people didn't get their stories from books – they were sung as musical poems. Because they are meant to convey information, ballads usually have a simple rhythm and a consistent rhyme scheme. They often tell the story of everyday heroes, and some poets, like Bob Dylan, continue to set them to music.

Blank Verse: Thanks to Shakespeare and others, blank verse is one of the most common forms of English poetry. It's verse that has no rhyme scheme but has a regular meter. Usually this meter is iambic pentameter (check out our definition below). Why is blank verse so common in English? Well, a lot of people think we speak in it in our everyday conversations. Kind of like we just did: "a LOT of PEO-ple THINK we SPEAK in IT." That could be a blank verse line.

Cadence: Cadence refers to the rhythmic or musical elements of a poem. You can think of it as the thing that makes poetry sound like poetry. Whereas "meter" refers to the regular elements of rhythm – the beats or accents – "cadence" refers to the momentary variations in rhythm, like when a line speeds up or slows down. Poets often repeat or contrast certain cadences to create a more interesting sound than normal prose.

Caesura: A fancy word for a pause that occurs in the middle of a line of verse. Use this if want to sound smart, but we think "pause" is just fine. You can create pauses in a lot of ways, but the most obvious is to use punctuation like a period, comma, or semicolon. Note that a pause at the end of a line is not a caesura.

Chiasmus: Chiasmus consists of two parallel phrases in which corresponding words or phrases are placed in the opposite order: "Fair is foul, foul is fair."

Cliché: Clichés are phrases or expressions that are used so much in everyday life, that people roll their eyes when they hear them. For example, "dead as a doornail" is a cliché. In good poetry, clichés are never used with a straight face, so if you see one, consider why the speaker might be using it.

Concrete Poetry: Concrete poetry conveys meaning by how it looks on the page. It's not a super-accurate term, and it can refer to a lot of different kinds of poems. One classic example is poems that look like they thing they describe. The French poet Guillaume Apollinaire wrote a poem about Paris in the shape of the Eiffel tower.

Connotation: The suggestive meaning of a word – the associations it brings up. The reason it's not polite to call a mentally-handicapped person "retarded" is that the word has a *negative* connotation. Connotations depend a lot on the culture and experience of the person reading the word. For some people, the word "liberal" has a positive connotation. For others, it's negative. Think of connotation as the murky haze hanging around the literal meaning of a word. Trying to figure out connotations of words can be one of the most confusing and fascinating aspects of reading poetry.

Contradiction: Two statements that don't seem to agree with each other. "I get sober when I drink alcohol" is a contradiction. Some contradictions, like "paradox" (see our definition below),

are only apparent, and they become true when you think about them in a certain way.

Denotation: The literal, straightforward meaning of a word. It's "dictionary definition." The word "cat" denotes an animal with four legs and a habit of coughing up furballs.

Dramatic Monologue: You can think of a dramatic monologue in poetry as a speech taken from a play that was never written. Okay, maybe that's confusing. It's a poem written in the voice of a fictional character and delivered to a fictional listener, instead of in the voice of a poet to his or her readers. The British poet Robert Browning is one of the most famous writers of . dramatic monologues. They are "dramatic" because they can be acted out, just like a play, and they are monologues because they consist of just one person speaking to another person, just as a "dialogue" consists of two people speaking. (The prefix "mono" means "one," whereas "di" means "two").

Elegy: An elegy is a poem about a dead person or thing. Whenever you see a poem with the title, "In Memory of . . .", for example, you're talking about an elegy. Kind of like that two-line poem you wrote for your pet rabbit Bubbles when you were five years old. Poor, poor Bubbles.

Ellipsis: You see ellipses all the time, usually in the form of "…". An ellipsis involves leaving out or suppressing words. It's like . . . well, you get the idea.

Enjambment: When a phrase carries over a line-break without a major pause. In French, the word means, "straddling," which we think is a perfect way to envision an enjambed line. Here's an example of enjambment from a poem by Joyce Kilmer: 'I think that I shall never see / A poem as lovely as a tree." The sentence continues right over the break with only a slight pause.

Extended metaphor: A central metaphor that acts like an "umbrella" to connect other metaphors or comparisons within it. It can span several lines or an entire poem. When one of Shakespeare's characters delivers an entire speech about how all the world is a stage and people are just actors, that's extended metaphor, with the idea of "theater" being the umbrella connecting everything.

Foot: The most basic unit of a poem's meter, a foot is a combination of long and short syllables. There are all kinds of different feet, such as "LONG-short" and "short-short-LONG." The first three words of the famous holiday poem, "'Twas the Night before Christmas," are one metrical foot (short-short-LONG). By far the most important foot to know is the iamb: short-LONG. An iamb is like one heartbeat: ba-DUM.

Free Verse: "Free bird! Play free bird!" Oops, we meant "Free verse! Define free verse!" Free verse is a poetic style that lacks a regular meter or rhyme scheme. This may sound like free verse has no style at all, but usually there is some recognizable consistency to the writer's use of rhythm. Walt Whitman was one of the pioneers of free verse, and nobody ever had trouble identifying a Whitman poem.

Haiku: A poetic form invented by the Japanese. In English, the haiku has three sections with five syllables, seven syllables, and five syllables respectively. They often describe natural imagery and include a word that reveals the season in which the poem is set. Aside from its

three sections, the haiku also traditionally features a sharp contrast between two ideas or images.

Heroic Couplet: Heroic couplets are rhyming pairs of verse in iambic pentameter. What on earth did this "couplets" do to become "heroic"? Did they pull a cat out of a tree or save an old lady from a burning building? In fact, no. They are called "heroic" because in the old days of English poetry they were used to talk about the trials and adventures of heroes. Although heroic couplets totally ruled the poetry scene for a long time, especially in the 17th and 18th centuries, nowadays they can sound kind of old-fashioned.

Hyperbole: A hyperbole is a gross exaggeration. For example, "tons of money" is a hyperbole.

Iambic Pentameter: Here it is, folks. Probably the single most useful technical term in poetry. Let's break it down: an "iamb" is an unaccented syllable followed by an accented one. "Penta" means "five," and "meter" refers to a regular rhythmic pattern. So "iambic pentameter" is a kind of *rhythmic pattern* that consist of *five iambs* per line. It's the most common rhythm in English poetry and sounds like five heartbeats: ba-DUM, ba-DUM, ba-DUM, ba-DUM, ba-DUM. Let's try it out on the first line of Shakespeare's *Romeo and Juliet*: "In fair Verona, where we lay our scene." Every second syllable is accented, so this is classic iambic pentameter.

Imagery: Imagery is intense, descriptive language in a poem that helps to trigger our senses and our memories when we read it.

Irony: Irony involves saying one thing while really meaning another, contradictory thing.

Metaphor: A metaphor happens when one thing is described as being another thing. "You're a toad!" is a metaphor – although not a very nice one. And metaphor is different from simile because it leaves out the words "like" or "as." For example, a simile would be, "You're *like* a toad."

Metonymy: Metonymy happens when some attribute of what is being described is used to indicate some other attribute. When talking about the power of a king, for example, one may instead say "the crown"-- that is, the physical attribute that is usually identified with royalty and power.

Ode: A poem written in praise or celebration of a person, thing, or event. Odes have been written about everything from famous battles and lofty emotions to family pets and household appliances. What would you write an ode about?

Onomatopoeia: Besides being a really fun word to say aloud, onomatopoeia refers either to words that resemble in sound what they represent. For example, do you hear the hissing noise when you say the word "hiss" aloud? And the old Batman television show *loved* onomatopoeia: "Bam! Pow! Kaplow!"

Oxymoron: An oxymoron is the combination of two terms ordinarily seen as opposites. For

example, "terribly good" is an oxymoron.

Paradox: A statement that contradicts itself and nonetheless seems true. It's a paradox when John Donne writes, "Death, thou shalt die," because he's using "death" in two different senses. A more everyday example might be, "Nobody goes to the restaurant because it's too crowded."

Parallelism: Parallelism happens a lot in poetry. It is the similarity of structure in a pair or series of related words, phrases, or clauses. Julius Caesar's famous words, "I came, I saw, I conquered," are an example of parallelism. Each clause begins with "I" and ends with a verb.

Pastoral: A poem about nature or simple, country life. If the poem you're reading features babbling brooks, gently swaying trees, hidden valleys, rustic haystacks, and sweetly singing maidens, you're probably dealing with a pastoral. The oldest English pastoral poems were written about the English countryside, but there are plenty of pastorals about the American landscape, too.

Personification: Personification involves giving human traits (qualities, feelings, action, or characteristics) to non-living objects (things, colors, qualities, or ideas).

Pun: A pun is a play on words. Puns show us the multiple meanings of a word by replacing that word with another that is similar in sound but has a very different meaning. For example, "when Shmoop went trick-or-treating in a Batman costume, he got lots of snickers." Hehe.

Quatrain: A stanza with four lines. Quatrains are the most common stanza form.

Refrain: A refrain is a regularly recurring phrase or verse especially at the end of each stanza or division of a poem or song. For example in T.S. Eliot's *Love Song for J. Alfred Prufrock*, the line, "in the room the women come and go / Talking of Michelangelo" is a refrain.

Rhetorical Question: Rhetorical questions involve asking a question for a purpose other than obtaining the information requested. For example, when we ask, "Shmoop, are you nuts?", we are mainly expressing our belief that Shmoop is crazy. In this case, we don't really expect Shmoop to tell us whether or not they are nuts.

Rhyming Couplet: A rhyming couplet is a pair of verses that rhyme. It's the simplest and most common rhyme scheme, but it can have more complicated variations (see "Heroic Couplet" for one example).

Simile: Similes compare one thing directly to another. For example, "My love is like a burning flame" is a simile. You can quickly identify similes when you see the words "like" or "as" used, as in "x is like y." Similes are different from metaphors – for example, a metaphor would refer to "the burning flame of my love."

Slam: A form of contemporary poetry that is meant to be performed at informal competitions rather than read. Slam readings are often very political in nature and draw heavily from the rhythms and energy of hip-hop music.

Slant Rhyme: A rhyme that isn't quite a rhyme. The words "dear" and "door" form a slant rhyme. The words sound similar, but they aren't close enough to make a full rhyme.

Sonnet: A well-known poetic form. Two of the most famous examples are the sonnets of William Shakespeare and John Donne. A traditional sonnet has fourteen lines in iambic pentameter and a regular rhyme scheme. Sonnets also feature a "turn" somewhere in the middle, where the poem takes a new direction or changes its argument in some way. This change can be subtle or really obvious. Although we English-speaking folks would love to take credit fort this amazing form, it was actually developed by the Italians and didn't arrive in England until the 16th century.

Speaker: The speaker is the voice *behind* the poem – the person we imagine to be speaking. It's important to note that the speaker is *not* the poet. Even if the poem is biographical, you should treat the speaker as a fictional creation, because the writer is choosing what to say about himself. Besides, even poets don't speak in poetry in their everyday lives – although it would be cool if they did.

Stanza: A division within a poem where a group of lines are formed into a unit. The word "stanza" comes from the Italian word for "room." Just like a room, a poetic stanza is set apart on a page by four "walls" of blank, white space.

Symbol: Generally speaking, a symbol is a sign representing something other than itself.

Synecdoche: In synecdoche a part of something represents the whole. For example: "One does not live by bread alone." The statement assumes that bread is representative of all categories of food.

Syntax: In technical terms, syntax is the study of how to put sentences together. In poetry, "syntax" refers to the way words and phrases relate to each other. Some poems have a syntax similar to everyday prose of spoken English (like the sentences you're reading right now). Other poems have a crazier syntax, where it's hard to see how things fit together at all. It can refer to the order of words in a sentence, like Yoda's wild syntax from the *Star Wars* movies: "A very important concept in poetry, syntax is!" Or, more figuratively, it can refer to the organization of ideas or topics in a poem: "Why did the poet go from talking about his mother to a description of an ostrich?"

Understatement: An understatement seeks to express a thought or impression by underemphasizing the extent to which a statement may be true. Understatement is the opposite of hyperbole and is frequently used for its comedic value in articles, speeches, etc. when issues of great importance are being discussed. Ex: "There's just one, tiny, little problem with that plan – it'll get us all killed!"

Sources:

http://allpoetry.com/column/2339540

http://academic.reed.edu/writing/paper_help/figurative_language.html
http://web.uvic.ca/wguide/Pages/LiteraryTermsTOC.html#RhetLang
http://www.tnellen.com/cybereng/lit_terms/allegory.html

1413182R0

Printed in Great Britain by
Amazon.co.uk, Ltd.,
Marston Gate.